I0448539

Contents

INTRODUCTION

An internal war is raging in Mexico between its government and the cartels who engage in corruption and terrorism to protect their sphere of influence and expand illegal operations. These criminals use wide-spread violence, assassination, kidnapping, extortion, and murder[1] to gain control over the flow of drugs, human trafficking, weapons, and money[2]. At the same time, the government of Mexico is grappling with a global economic recession, a substantial decline in the country's known oil reserves[3] and growing environmental problems (desertification, water availability and soil erosion).[4] If the situation continues to deteriorate, the United States may be asked to assist the government of Mexico in a variety of roles.

Personnel assigned to work in Mexico will be exposed to a complex and wide array of environmental hazards that will require robust counter measures. When environmental hazards are not promptly identified and addressed, disease, disability or death can result. Yet history has shown that unintended exposures to environmental hazards continue to occur despite best efforts. Using the U.S. military's experience as an example, commanders are charged with minimizing adverse health effects while maximizing operational effectiveness[5] and they have at their disposal well-developed doctrine, organizations and processes that support force sustainment. Yet although progress has been made to improve deployment health activities, there are still opportunities for improvement. The U.S. must strengthen its risk mitigation strategy for environmental hazards before sending personnel to assist Mexico.

This paper is a starting point for further study about the types of environmental hazards in Mexico and the potential health impact. It uses examples from past U.S. military exposures, along with insights on emerging issues, to illustrate why an effective risk mitigation strategy is essential. A technique is proposed for enhancing the mitigation process.

BACKGROUND

Mitigation is defined as reducing the possibility that a risk event will occur or reducing the impact if a risk event happens.[6] It means examining root causes and the interactions between risks so an effective strategy can be developed.[7] Inadequate or untimely mitigation of environmental hazards can lead to debilitating health problems and make it more difficult to achieve overall objectives.

Department of Defense (DoD) policy requires the completion of an overall health risk assessment for each Area of Operation (AO) before deployment in order to identify health threats and protective measures (such as medications, immunizations, or personal protective equipment). DoD Instruction Number 6490.03, dated August 2006, states the objective is "to anticipate, identify, and assess health threats; develop controls and countermeasures; make risk decisions; and implement controls to mitigate unavoidable health threats."[8] Yet, two years later, a RAND study for the Army identified several vulnerabilities in the risk management process. This research paper argues that environmental health threats in Mexico are significant enough to warrant development of an improved type of mitigation plan that takes into account lessons learned and emerging threats to develop pre-emptive actions.

Environmental hazards can be naturally occurring, infectious, or man-made. *Natural* hazards in Mexico include hurricanes, earthquakes, tsunamis, volcanic eruptions, mudslides, floods, desertification, and wildfires.[9] *Infectious* hazards in Mexico pose an intermediate risk of disease and include food or waterborne illness, hepatitis, dengue fever, Valley Fever, West Nile virus, and malaria, among others.[10] *Man-made* environmental hazards include air and water pollution, unsanitary and untreated wastes, chemical contamination, and uncontrolled radioactive sources. The focus of this paper is on man-made environmental hazards.

DISCUSSION / ANALYSIS

Experts may say that, even though the challenges have been daunting, Mexico has made real progress towards improving the environment. In 1992, the United Nations named Mexico City the most polluted city on earth. Its air was so toxic that birds died while in flight.[11] The Mexican capital's air pollution hospitalized more than a million people in 1999.[12] Pollution control measures that started in the mid-1980s eventually began to produce positive results. Since 1990, air carbon monoxide levels in Mexico City have been greatly reduced, while concentrations of lead and particulates decreased by 90% and 70%, respectively.[13] In addition, plans were finalized to remediate more than 300 contaminated sites across Mexico by providing loans to landowners to hire contractors for clean up.[14]

On the U.S.-Mexico border, efforts to improve the unhealthy environment have been in place for nearly 30 years. In 1983, U.S. and Mexico signed the La Paz agreement which was the first mutual attempt to address pollution and hazardous materials on the border.[15] In 1992, the Integrated Border Environmental Plan promoted compliance with existing regulations, encouraged investment in infrastructure, and established cooperative planning and training. In 1995-2000, the Border XXI Program provided technical assistance, training, and technology upgrades. Under the Border 2012 Program (2003-2012), progress was made in air quality, access to drinking water and sanitation, and contaminant removal. The draft Border 2020 plan will expand to include e-waste, waste reduction, and recycling.[16]

Yet even though Mexico has done remarkably well in reversing some of its worst environmental damage, the country has a long way to go before the health threat is reduced to a level that is acceptable by U.S. standards. Hazards are numerous which partly explains why the residents of Mexico experience more ailments than would otherwise be expected.

Advocates for the status quo might assert that it doesn't matter whether Mexico's environment presents dangerous health risks since the U.S. will counter the threat through its existing hazard surveillance and risk management programs. It could also be argued that DoD learned lessons from Viet Nam and the Persian Gulf which have been used to correct deficiencies in risk mitigation. Indeed, progress has been made in four major areas.

Surveillance: DoD has capitalized on the internet to provide on-line environmental sampling data and near real-time monitoring capability. The data and other tools are used to determine operational risk, develop recommendations, and investigate adverse health outcomes.[17] In 2001-2008, more than 17,500 samples were collected in multiple theaters.[18]

Guidance: The military continues to update doctrine and technical manuals pertaining to environmental hazards. Written guidelines establish the requirement to include environmental considerations in operational plans and orders[19] in order to reduce potential and actual exposures as much as possible while still accomplishing the mission.[20]

Process: In October 2009, DoD officials assured Congress that there has been significant improvement its ability to identify and prevent or limit possible exposures using rigorous risk management.[21] For example, the U.S. military identified the location of physical and industrial hazards across Afghanistan to examine troop health concerns.[22]

Record Keeping: Daily recording of location was implemented to help track those individuals who might have been exposed to environmental hazards. In addition, base camp hazards are more thoroughly documented.[23]

While acknowledging that important advancements have been made to develop more sophisticated decision-support tools, procedures and monitoring capabilities that facilitate Force Health Protection[24], there is room for improvement as detailed later in this paper.

ENVIRONMENTAL HAZARDS IN MEXICO

Although Mexico has made true progress towards improving its environment, multiple health hazards remain a threat. Rapid population and industrial growth has outpaced Mexico's infrastructure and pollution controls, particularly in urban areas and on the northern border. Many residents of Mexico have contracted illnesses due to environmental degradation with indigenous communities and informal settlements at most risk.[25] Personnel working in Mexico can expect to encounter areas plagued by dangerous levels of air and water pollution, improperly treated solid waste, pesticides, raw sewage, chemical contaminants, hazardous waste or disease.

Air Pollution: The Mexican Health Secretariat said that over a third of Mexico's disease burden is due to environmental factors, with air pollution the most significant.[26] In 2011, the U.S. Environmental Protection Agency (EPA) listed the high concentration of particulates, ozone, and toxic pollutants in the air as a major health concern in several border communities.[27] Inhaled particulates can lead to diminished lung function, worsening of respiratory and heart diseases, or premature death. Ozone can also damage lung tissue.[28] Although Mexico City is no longer the most polluted city on earth, it has the worst air pollution in the nation and is in the top thirty globally.[29] Mexico's second largest city, Guadalajara, surpassed air pollution limits 90% of the year in 2008.[30] Mexico struggles to retain its environmental gains as the number of people, industries, and vehicles increase.

Water Pollution: The government of Mexico has identified the lack of clean water as a national security concern.[31] As recently as September 2011, the EPA cited lack of access to safe drinking water as a significant public health threat in border communities.[32] Nationally, most of the population has access to potable water but only 45% had an uninterrupted supply according to the 2000 census. The rest receive water once a day or intermittently during the week. In 2005, there were nearly 6 million cases of diarrheic diseases resulting in over 4,200 deaths (equivalent to 4 deaths per 1,000 inhabitants) of which 60% may be attributable to water contamination.[33]

Sewage: Inadequate sanitation coverage can spread infectious diseases. In 2005, only 35% of the total sewage generated and collected in municipal systems was treated.[34] In rural Mexico, 32% of the population lacks improved sanitation facilities.[35]

Hazardous Waste: Mexico has a scarcity of hazardous waste disposal facilities[36] and inadequate collection and treatment. Less than half of the 10 million tons of hazardous waste produced annually by industry is disposed of correctly.[37] The remainder is stored on site or illegally dumped. As the number of manufacturing plants on the border continues to rise, chemical emergencies have become more frequent (700 reported incidents in 2003-2005).[38]

Pesticides: Mexico used DDT for over 40 years until the practice was stopped in 2002.[39] DDT is a known carcinogen which can remain active in soil or water for 30 years. Since DDT toxins persist in the environment for such a lengthy period, legacy contamination is an ongoing concern. After DDT was discontinued, Mexico moved towards safer pesticides, but in 2010 it was reported that some fumigators are switching back to controversial or carcinogenic chemicals because the mosquito which transmits dengue has developed resistance.[40] Agricultural use of pesticides is widespread in Mexico.[41]

Solid Waste: In 2008, 77% of solid waste was collected but only 35% was disposed of under sanitary conditions.[42] Industrial waste is often inappropriately handled in the same manner as domestic waste, contaminating groundwater with toxic chemicals.[43]

Infectious Disease: There are many infectious diseases in Mexico and inadequate environmental controls increase the rate of disease. Climate change has created warmer conditions more favorable for the spread of dengue.[44] The hemorrhagic form of dengue can be fatal if left untreated[45] and no vaccine is available, making early recognition critical.[46] Malaria, always serious and potentially deadly, is present in various parts of Mexico.

Radiation: Mexico has one nuclear power plant with 2 reactors in Veracruz.[47] There is intense speculation in the local area regarding whether the facility poses a recurring health risk.[48] A 2008 simulation concluded that 80% of Mexico would be affected by a nuclear accident at the site.[49] Mexico's 2011-2015 Country Program Framework lists radioactive waste disposal and environmental protection among its priorities.[50] The worst radiation accident in Mexican history occurred in the mid-1980s when a smuggled, unregistered radiotherapy machine containing Cobalt-60 was junked and unknowingly reprocessed into iron components that ended up in over 17,600 buildings across 16 of Mexico's states.[51]

It is unlikely that Mexico's environmental problems will be satisfactorily corrected in the near term. Compliance with environmental laws is lax due to corruption and the relatively small number of enforcement officers. The government is more likely to focus on the economy and cartel violence than environmental protection. Investors can be expected to continue the past practice of funding manufacturing, trade, and industrial projects that attract foreign currency rather than investing in pollution controls and waste management.[52] Illegal dumping will persist until more treatment facilities are built and disposal costs decrease.[53]

The data highlights the significance of Mexico's environmental problems and supports the assertion that the health threats in this region have broad scope and complexity, with the potential for tragic medical outcomes in the absence of a risk mitigation strategy.

EXPOSURES DURING PAST DEPLOYMENTS

Despite the U.S. military's best efforts, history has shown that unintended exposures to environmental health hazards continue to occur. As a result, large numbers of personnel are presumed to have been harmed during deployment. Future risk mitigation efforts can be strengthened by learning from past deployments, especially as it pertains to identifying root causes or patterns of risk that facilitate a systems approach. Below is a partial list of exposures that occurred between 1962 and the present.

Agent Orange: Veterans who served in Vietnam from Jan 9, 1962 to May 7, 1975 may have been exposed to Agent Orange, a mix of herbicides used to destroy crops and remove foliage that concealed enemy forces.[54] Individuals who came into contact with the defoliant outside of Vietnam may also be affected. The risk is greatest to those who loaded Agent Orange on to aircraft or stored, mixed or dispensed the chemical.[55] This population has higher rates of cancer, Parkinson's disease, leukemia, lymphoma, diabetes, and other illnesses.[56] In 1984, a class-action lawsuit led to the biggest monetary settlement of its kind.[57]

Gulf War Illness: VA defines Gulf War Veterans as personnel on active duty in Southwest Asia any time between August 2, 1990 to the present (during the first Gulf War, the Iraq War or subsequent operations). It includes Desert Shield, Desert Storm, Iraqi Freedom and New Dawn. This population may have been exposed to multiple environmental hazards and potentially harmful substances such as burn pits in Afghanistan and Iraq, biological and chemical warfare agents, depleted uranium (used in tank armor and some types of projectiles), pesticides, oil well fires and petroleum, pyridostigmine bromide pills, and certain vaccinations. VA presumes that chronic, medically unexplained multi-symptom illnesses are related to Gulf War service without regard to cause. Medically Unexplained

Symptoms (MUS) include fatigue, joint pain, indigestion, insomnia, dizziness, headaches, and memory problems, among others.[58]

OEF/OIF: Operation Enduring Freedom (OEF) and Operation Iraqi Freedom (OIF) personnel may have been exposed to depleted uranium, toxic embedded fragments, rabies, CARC paint, Chromium at Qarmat Ali Water Treatment Facility, and other hazards.[59] A fire at Mishraq Sulfur Mine near Mosul, Iraq in 2003 exposed 2,500-3,000 troops to sulfur dioxide and hydrogen sulfide[60] resulting in cases of constrictive bronchiolitis.[61] In 2004, industrial air pollution and unpredictable chemical releases at Ash Shuaiba Port in Kuwait caused troops to become ill from pollution, and ammonia or sulfur dioxide emissions.[62] In Southwest Asia, exposure may have resulted from inhalation of fine sand and dust[63] since hazard surveillance identified significant, breathable particulate matter in the air at concentrations five times higher than the standard. The long-term health effect is unknown.[64]

Japan: In 1985-2001, a waste incinerator near Naval Air Facility Atsugi generated pollutants that have been identified as a possible hazard since the rate of respiratory problems and cancer is higher.[65] For 15 years, the incinerator burned construction debris, solid and liquid industrial waste, and municipal solid waste which generated toxic smoke that drifted over the base. About 18,000 adults and 8,000 children were potentially exposed.[66]

Bosnia: In 1996, the army placed a base camp between a caustic soda plant and a cement plant. Air pollution from the facilities turned into caustic ash that peeled paint off vehicles and sickened soldiers. The base camp was quickly moved to a better area.[67]

Infectious Diseases: VA presumes certain diseases are related to service in Southwest Asia or Afghanistan: Malaria, Brucellosis, Campylobacter Jejuni, Q Fever, Non-Typhoid Salmonella, Mycobacterium Tuberculosis, Leishmaniasis, Shigella and West Nile Virus.[68]

A review of these and other environmental incidents identified the following themes:

- *Some military personnel were exposed to the same hazard for years without effective risk mitigation.* As an illustrative example, open burn pits were widely used in Iraq and Afghanistan from 2001 until 2009. Burn pits were often placed near base camps or encroached upon camps. In October 2009, legislation was passed that banned burns pits during contingency operations unless no alternative exists. Legislators expressed concern about DoD's inconsistent approach which recommended locating burn pits far away from base camps while also asserting there is no health risk.[69]

- *Some individuals unwittingly exposed themselves to hazards due to lack of awareness or inadequate training*, as when troops in Iraq were sickened while rolling drums to clear out a building. They did not realize the leaking barrels contained industrial-grade pesticides.[70]

- *Risk identification was not always proactive*, as when soldiers in Afghanistan were put in housing containing friable asbestos; prolonged exposure to asbestos can cause lung cancer.[71]

- *Inadequate resources can lead to exposures*, as occurred when a lack of mosquito control equipment at a base camp in Southwest Asia resulted in multiple mosquito breeding sites.[72]

- *Risk mitigation occurred but was untimely.* In 2003, for example, 830 service members at a water treatment plant in Qarmat Ali, Iraq were exposed to a carcinogen (hexavalent chromium). Although exposure began in the spring, the contaminated ground wasn't cleaned and covered with asphalt until September.[73]

Environmental risks that are not adequately managed can jeopardize the mission or result in negative publicity, lawsuits, political outrage, expensive consequence management, and long-term healthcare costs.[74] History shows that if risk mitigation is absent, ineffective or delayed, environmental health threats can have potentially devastating consequences.

ANTICIPATING EMERGING ISSUES

Risk mitigation efforts are strengthened by knowing the region well enough to anticipate emerging environmental hazards. Further, creative thinking is required to avoid being caught off-guard by unexpected risks. Emerging environmental hazards in Mexico include illegal drug contaminants, nanotechnology, cement kilns, and defoliants.

Illegal Drug Contaminants: Mexico is the leading foreign supplier of marijuana (cannabis) and methamphetamine to the United States.[75] Cannabis cultivation is associated with illegal dumpsites of highly toxic repellants and insecticides that poison water sources and kill wildlife.[76] Methamphetamine and its precursors (explosives, solvents, salts, metals and corrosives) can be even more dangerous than cannabis dumps, causing meth production facilities to ignite or explode.[77] Exposure to high levels of toxic fumes and chemicals in meth labs can result in severe burns, lung damage[78] or even death.[79] Meth labs can be found anywhere; in residential areas, motel rooms, garages, sheds, camp sites, and vehicles.[80] For each pound of meth produced, 5 to 7 pounds of hazardous waste is generated. The waste is usually left on-site or it is dumped in sewers, backyards, ditches, fields or streams.[81] People have become ill from picking up roadside litter[82] and abandoned meth labs exhibit residual toxicity until surfaces, fabrics, air ducts and drains are professionally cleaned.[83] This implies that personnel could be put at risk simply by renting a hotel room or jogging beside a road. Thousands of bags and hundreds of barrels filled with meth and its precursors are regularly seized in ports and warehouses by Mexican forces. An elaborate underground meth lab with tunnel access was discovered on July 20, 2011. On the same day in another location, 926 tons of precursors were found.[84] The Mexican drug cartels adapt to disruptions in the precursor supply chain by identifying substitutes, altering the type of health threat that is posed.

11

Nanotechnology: Within the Latin American region, Brazil, Argentina and Mexico are leaders in nanotechnology research and development; however, Mexico is the only one that lacks a national plan. Mexico has entered into multiple nanotechnology agreements with research centers, foreign universities, and overseas industries to expand its capabilities. The concern is that without a plan, risks may be completely ignored in the rush to obtain patents or capture market share.[85] Nanotechnology is an applied science that engineers structures, devices, and systems by manipulating the shape and size of matter at the nanoscale (100 nm down to the size of atoms).[86] Since they are so small, nanoparticles that are inhaled, ingested, or absorbed through the skin have the potential to cause harm. Research is still ongoing, so the actual risk is currently unknown. However, there is mounting evidence that exposure to certain engineered nanoparticles results in adverse health effects in lab animals.[87] Improper storage and disposal could result in a new type of environmental pollution.[88] Nanotechnology applications are currently limited but include food production, electronics, military weapons, sensors, cosmetics, drugs, paint, chemicals, pesticides, clothing and medical devices.[89]

Cement Kilns: Mexico has started to let cement kilns burn hazardous waste as fuel instead of coal, natural gas and oil.[90] The hazardous fuel includes solvents, tires, paint, rubber, plastics and dyes. The change was made to promote recycling, reduce use of fossil fuels[91] and lower operating costs to gain a commercial advantage.[92] Cement kilns are generally not required to meet the stricter emission standards expected of a hazardous waste incinerator. The result is an increase in the amount and toxicity of air emissions, which are spread by wind to water and soil where they are absorbed into the food chain. The heavy metals produced (arsenic and lead, for example) contaminate the cement and cement powder that is sent to market. The kiln's dust and ash are hazardous, requiring special disposal. The health threat from burning hazardous waste in cement kilns is serious and the contaminants can persist for decades.[93] (This hazard is reminiscent of the Atsugi Japan case on page 9.)

Defoliants: The U.S. Border Patrol planned to spray the herbicide imazapyr from helicopters along the banks of the Rio Grande River on the U.S.-Mexico border to remove foliage that conceals drug smugglers and illegal immigrants. The $2 million pilot project was to start on March 25, 2009 but was suspended after local governments in both countries grew concerned about possible drinking water contamination. The public was alarmed due to the plan's similarity to the Agent Orange defoliation strategy used in Vietnam. If the pilot is successful, the initiative will expand along the border.[94] A lawsuit was filed to obtain federal intervention, alleging the Border Patrol failed to assess the environmental impact.[95] Although the EPA said "there is a reasonable certainty that no harm will result,"[96] Border Patrol decided to delay spraying until further investigation is conducted on the health effects.[97]

The examples above demonstrate that emerging environmental hazards can and should be anticipated to facilitate the development of proactive risk mitigation strategies. Unfortunately, the preventive medicine and medical personnel who identify and assess health hazards might miss important warning signs if too much emphasis is placed on repeating the type of analysis that worked in the past. The spread of automation and internet databases to collect hazard surveillance data provides consistent, accessible and real-time information. A drawback, however, is the temptation to allow computer templates to artificially define the boundaries of an issue during problem framing. In order to help decision-makers plan for known hazards as well as hazards that aren't on anyone's radar yet, the risk mitigation process should be based on a good understanding of the environmental landscape and involve the identification of risks and emerging issues along with root causes and inter-relationships.

13

RISK MITIGATION EXERCISE

The following analysis, although superficial, is included for illustrative purposes to demonstrate how the risk mitigation approach proposed in this paper might strengthen the existing process. It also suggests why risk mitigation needs advance preparation time in order to be effective.

OBJECTIVE: Develop a mitigation strategy for Mexico that will either reduce the possibility that a significant environmental risk event will occur or reduce the impact if a risk event happens.

STEP ONE: Using knowledge of the environmental landscape, identify current environmental hazards. In Mexico, the current environmental risks include infectious diseases, air and water pollution, unsanitary and untreated wastes, chemical contamination, and uncontrolled radioactive sources as detailed above.

STEP TWO: Using knowledge of the environmental landscape and creative thinking, identify emerging environmental hazards. Mexico's emerging environmental risks include illegal drug contaminants, nanotechnology, cement kilns, and defoliants.

STEP THREE: Examine root causes and the relationship between risks. A cursory review indicates three out of four of Mexico's emerging hazards have something in common. In each case, the desire for financial gain took, or would probably take, precedence over environmental responsibility. In the fourth case, a U.S. government agency put crime fighting and border protection ahead of the environment. Two of the emerging hazards were similar to historical cases that led to serious health effects in some personnel (Agent Orange and Atsugi Japan). Many of the current hazards are due to inadequate infrastructure or improper waste disposal methods and are most problematic along the U.S.-Mexico border, in the largest cities, and in areas with indigenous populations or informal settlements. Infectious diseases are made more likely due to pesticide-resistant disease vectors and areas of inadequate sanitation.

STEP FOUR: Develop an effective Risk Mitigation Strategy. Based on the above, some pre-emptive counter measures would be: 1) Pre-deployment training on how to identify a meth lab and storage facilities along with the dangers, preventive health techniques, and consequence management training; 2) Same as #1 but for cannabis-related chemical waste dumps; 3) Since the health risk from nanotechnology is currently unknown but lab animal testing suggests there may be a hazard, obtain the most recent update on the risk from the research community. Identify the location of nanotechnology and nanomaterial manufacturers and their waste sites to avoid placing base camps nearby; 4) Obtain intelligence on the location of cement kilns and avoid locating base camps nearby; 5) Work with U.S. Border Patrol to obtain their schedule for defoliant spraying and avoid operations in that area; 6) Work with Mexico to incentivize environmentally responsible behavior in the business community as a long-term objective; 7) Identify the location of areas with limited access to clean water, sewage disposal, or solid waste disposal and plan for appropriate precautions; 8) Same as #7 for areas with severe air pollution or toxic emissions; 9) Identify the location of hazardous waste dumps to avoid placing base camps nearby.

The risk mitigation technique outlined here is proposed to strengthen existing processes in order to avoid unintended exposures to environmental hazards to the extent possible. The key is to proactively plan for hazards that are known, as well as the unexpected, using knowledge of the environment, creativity and critical thinking skills.

15

CONCLUSIONS

On October 8, 2009 at a Senate Veterans Affairs Committee hearing, legislators heard about military exposures to contaminants. Two major conclusions were drawn: 1) There is a general lack of knowledge about environmental hazards during deployment and 2) There is a lack of knowledge about health consequences following deployment.[98] This assessment was delivered a year after a RAND study[99] for the Army cited vulnerabilities in environmental risk management, and it was three years after DoD Instruction Number 6490.03 reminded all Services of the responsibility to identify and mitigate deployment health threats. History shows that despite the U.S. military's best efforts, unintended exposures to environmental health hazards can and do occur. As a result, some personnel are presumed to have been harmed during deployment. Without question, DoD has made steady improvement in its ability to identify and prevent or limit possible exposures and its capabilities are robust. However, there is still an opportunity for improvement.

The environmental hazards in Mexico are complex, widespread, and significant enough to warrant the proactive development of an effective risk mitigation plan. Current hazards include infectious diseases, air and water pollution, unsanitary and untreated wastes, chemical contamination, and uncontrolled radioactive sources. Emerging environmental hazards include illegal drug contaminants, nanotechnology, cement kilns, and defoliants. The ideal risk mitigation process would also take into account lessons learned from history, root causes, and the relationship between risks to develop appropriate countermeasures. Creativity and critical thinking is essential to avoid being caught off-guard. Although time consuming, the development of risk mitigation strategies is worth the effort in order to prevent debilitating, sometimes fatal, health problems while maximizing operational effectiveness.

RECOMMENDATIONS

This study identified four areas where more research is needed in order to develop an effective risk mitigation strategy for environmental hazards in Mexico:

1. Conduct additional study about the environmental hazards of Mexico to supplement the work done so far. It should include the identification and analysis of current and emerging environmental risks, their root causes and interactions, and trends.

2. Obtain aggregated health data for the population consisting of Mexico's active duty service members and veterans to determine whether mortality and morbidity is higher in those groups. If so, can the increased rate of disease be linked to environmental hazard exposures?

3. Determine whether Mexico's army has any best practices for mitigating the risk of environmental hazards in the region and share the lessons learned.

4. Identify ways to enhance the current risk mitigation process in order to prevent unwanted exposures to environmental hazards. Go beyond prophylactic or protective measures to develop creative, pre-emptive actions that will help avoid or eliminate the risks.

It is hoped this information will stimulate further thought to help protect U.S. personnel should the need arise to assist in Mexico or elsewhere.

NOTES

1. Barry R. McCaffrey and Robert H. Scales, *Texas Border Security: A Strategic Military Assessment* (Colgen LP, 2011), Attachment 12, 7.
2. Ibid., p. 22.
3. U.S. Department of State. *Background Note: Mexico*, 14 December 2010, http://www.state.gov/r/pa/ei/bgn/35749.htm (accessed 9 October 2011).
4. Global Security.org, "Environment," *Global Security.org*, 7 September 2011, http://www.globalsecurity.org/military/world/mexico/environment.htm (accessed 10 October 2011).
5. David E. Mosher, et. al., *Green Warriors - Army Environmental Considerations for Contingency Operations from Planning Through Post-Conflict* (Santa Monica, CA: RAND, 2008), 36.
6. National Research Council, *The Owner's Role in Project Risk Management*, (The National Academies Press, 2005), Chapter 5.
7. Ibid.
8. U.S. Department of Defense, *"DOD Instruction Number 6490.03, Deployment Health,"* (Washington, DC: Department of Defense, 11 August 2006).
9. Central Intelligence Agency, "The World Factbook: Mexico," CIA, 27 September 2011, https://www.cia.gov/library/publications/the-world-factbook/geos/mx.html (accessed 9 October 2011).
10. Ibid.
11. Anne-Marie O'Connor, "Mexico City Drastically Reduced Air Pollutants Since 1990s," *The Washington Post*, 1 April 2010, http://www.washingtonpost.com/wp-dyn/content/article/2010/03/31/AR2010033103614.html?sid=ST2010033103622/ (accessed 12 October 2011).
12. Advameg Inc., "Environment," 2007, http://www.city-data.com/world-cities/Mexico-City-Environment.html (accessed 9 October 2011).
13. Anne-Marie O'Connor, "Mexico City Drastically Reduced Air Pollutants Since 1990s," *The Washington Post*, 1 April 2010, http://www.washingtonpost.com/wp-dyn/content/article/2010/03/31/AR2010033103614.html?sid=ST2010033103622 (accessed 12 October 2011).
14. U.S. Commercial Service, " Environmental Services in Mexico," Klean Industries, 14 October 2008, http://www.kleanindustries.com/s/PressReleases.asp?ReportID=325076 (accessed 9 October 2011).
15. Dean E. Carter, et. al., "Environmental Health and Hazardous Waste Issues Related to the U.S.-Mexico Border," (*Environmental Health Perspectives*, Vol. 104, Number 6, June 1996), 591.
16. Environmental Protection Agency, *Border 2020: U.S.-Mexico Environmental Program*, draft for public comment (EPA, 15 September 2011).
17. U.S. Army Public Health Command, Deployment Environmental Surveillance Program (DESP), http://phc.amedd.army.mil/organization/institute/dhrm/Pages/DESP.aspx (accessed 12 October 2011).
18. U.S. Medicine, "Legislators Express Concern Regarding Environmental Hazards," *U.S. Medicine*, November 2009, http://www.usmedicine.com/articles/legislators-express-concern-regarding-environmental-hazards.html / (accessed 8 October 2011).
19. David E. Mosher, et. al., *Green Warriors - Army Environmental Considerations for Contingency Operations from Planning Through Post-Conflict* (Santa Monica, CA: RAND, 2008), 53.

20. U.S. Army Personnel Health Command, *Environmental Health Risk Assessment and Chemical Exposure Guidelines for Deployed Military Personnel (TG 230),* (Department of the Army, 2010.

21. U.S. Medicine, "Legislators Express Concern Regarding Environmental Hazards," *U.S. Medicine,* November 2009, http://www.usmedicine.com/articles/legislators-express-concern-regarding-environmental-hazards.html / (accessed 8 October 2011).

22. David E. Mosher, et. al., *Green Warriors - Army Environmental Considerations for Contingency Operations from Planning Through Post-Conflict* (Santa Monica, CA: RAND, 2008), 194.

23. U.S. Medicine, "Legislators Express Concern Regarding Environmental Hazards," *U.S. Medicine,* November 2009, http://www.usmedicine.com/articles/legislators-express-concern-regarding-environmental-hazards.html / (accessed 8 October 2011).

24. U.S. Army Public Health Command, Deployment Environmental Surveillance Program (DESP), http://phc.amedd.army.mil/organization/institute/dhrm/Pages/DESP.aspx (accessed 12 October 2011).

25. Environmental Protection Agency, *Border 2020: U.S.-Mexico Environmental Program*, draft for public comment (EPA, 15 September 2011).

26. Oil and Gas Author, Environmental Issues in Mexico, 24 August 2006. http://www.oilgasarticles.com/articles/212/1/Environmental-Issues-in-Mexico/Page1.html (accessed 9 August 2011).

27. Environmental Protection Agency, *Border 2020: U.S.-Mexico Environmental Program*, draft for public comment (EPA, 15 September 2011).

28. Environmental Protection Agency, *State of the Border Region - Indicators Report 2005,* EPA-160-R-06-001, (EPA, 2006), 10.

29. Blacksmith Institute, *The World's Worst Polluted Places: The Top Ten of the Dirty Thirty*, 2007, http://www.blacksmithinstitute.org/wwpp2007/finalReport2007.pdf, (accessed 9 October 2011).

30. U.S. Commercial Service, " Environmental Services in Mexico," Klean Industries, 14 October 2008, http://www.kleanindustries.com/s/PressReleases.asp?ReportID=325076 (accessed 9 October 2011).

31. Central Intelligence Agency, "The World Factbook: Mexico," CIA, 27 September 2011, https://www.cia.gov/library/publications/the-world-factbook/geos/mx.html (accessed 9 October 2011).

32. Environmental Protection Agency, *Border 2020: U.S.-Mexico Environmental Program*, draft for public comment (EPA, 15 September 2011).

33. Boris Maranon-Pimentel, "Economic Costs of Water-related Health Problems in Mexico: Deficiencies in Potable Water Services and the Costs of Treatment of Diarrhoeas." *Water Resources Development, Vol. 25, No. 1, 65–80*, March 2009.

34. Ibid.

35. Central Intelligence Agency, "The World Factbook: Mexico," CIA, 27 September 2011, https://www.cia.gov/library/publications/the-world-factbook/geos/mx.html (accessed 9 October 2011).

36. Ibid.

37. U.S. Commercial Service, " Environmental Services in Mexico," Klean Industries, 14 October 2008, http://www.kleanindustries.com/s/PressReleases.asp?ReportID=325076 (accessed 9 October 2011).

38. Environmental Protection Agency, *U.S.-Mexico Environmental Program: Border 2012, Implementation and Mid-Term Report* (EPA, 2007). http://www.epa.gov/usmexicoborder/docs/implementation_2007_eng.pdf: EPA, 2007.

39. Barbara Sibbald, "DDT Use Finally Eliminated in North America," *Canadian Medical Association Journal,* Vol. 166, No. 10, May 14, 2002.

40. New Mexico State University, "Dengue on the Loose," *Frontera NorteSur*, 25 July 2010. http://fnsnews.nmsu.edu/2010/07/25/dengue-on-the-loose/ (accessed 11 October 2011).

41. Environmental Protection Agency, State of the Border Region Indicators Report 2005, EPA, 20 March 2007, http://epa.gov/border2012/indicators/water.html (accessed 9 October 2011).

42. U.S. Commercial Service, " Environmental Services in Mexico," Klean Industries, 14 October 2008, http://www.kleanindustries.com/s/PressReleases.asp?ReportID=325076 (accessed 9 October 2011).

43. Environmental Protection Agency, "Environmental Pollution," Oracle Education Foundation, 1998, http://library.thinkquest.org/C001611/pollution.html (accessed 10 October 2011).

44. New Mexico State University, "Dengue on the Loose," *Frontera NorteSur*, 25 July 2010. http://fnsnews.nmsu.edu/2010/07/25/dengue-on-the-loose/ (accessed 11 October 2011).

45. Centers for Disease Control and Prevention, *Dengue in Tropical and Subtropical Regions*, 15 September 2011. http://wwwnc.cdc.gov/travel/notices/outbreak-notice/dengue-tropical-sub-tropical.htm (accessed 19 October 2011).

46. Ibid.

47. John Ross, "Dangers in Paradise - Environmental Problems in Mexico," *Sierra*, July-Aug 1992, http://findarticles.com/p/articles/mi_m1525/is_n4_v77/ai_12449677/ (accessed 10 October 2011).

48. Emilio Godoy, "Villagers Complain of Health Risks from Nuclear Plant," *Inter Press Service (IPS).* 30 March 2011, http://ipsnews.net/news.asp?idnews=55060 (accessed 10 October 2011).

49. Ibid.

50. Emilio Godoy, "Mexico: Little Oversight of Radiation Sources," *Global Issues*, 13 May 2011. http://www.globalissues.org/news/2011/05/13/9648 (accessed 10 October 2011).

51. Ibid.

52. George Kourous, "Environmental Problems and Cross-border Activism," *Information Services Latin America (ISLA).* 1999. http://isla.igc.org/Features/Border/mex3.html (accessed 9 October 2011).

53. Ibid.

54. VA Public Health, Hazardous Exposures, Department of Veterans Affairs, 29 September 2011, http://www.publichealth.va.gov/exposures/index.asp (accessed 8 October 2011).

55. American Cancer Society, *Agent Orange and Cancer,*25 June 2010. http://www.cancer.org/Cancer/CancerCauses/OtherCarcinogens/IntheWorkplace/agent-orange-and-cancer (accessed October 11, 2011).

56. VA Public Health, *When and Where Agent Orange Was Sprayed in Vietnam*, 19 August 2011, http://www.publichealth.va.gov/exposures/agentorange/diseases.asp#veterans (accessed 24 October 2011).

57. Veterans Benefits Administration, *The Agent Orange Settlement Fund.* 8 November 2009, http://www.vba.va.gov/bln/21/benefits/herbicide/AOno2.htm (accessed 25 October 2011).

58. VA Public Health, *Gulf War Veterans' Illnesses*, Department of Veterans Affairs, 15 September 2011. http://www.publichealth.va.gov/exposures/gulfwar/index.asp (accessed 11 October 2011).

59. VA Public Health, Operations Enduring Freedom and Iraqi Freedom (OEF/OIF) Hazardous Exposures, 19 May 2011, http://www.publichealth.va.gov/exposures/oefoif/index.asp (accessed 11 October 2011).

60. George P. Johnson, "Deployment Health and Environmental Exposures in OEF/OIF," Power Point, 29 January 2007. www.tricare.mil/conferences/2007/Mon/M109.ppt (accessed 21 October 2011).

61. U.S. Medicine, "Legislators Express Concern Regarding Environmental Hazards," *U.S. Medicine*, November 2009, http://www.usmedicine.com/articles/legislators-express-concern-regarding-environmental-hazards.html / (accessed 8 October 2011).

62. David E. Mosher, et. al., *Green Warriors - Army Environmental Considerations for Contingency Operations from Planning Through Post-Conflict* (Santa Monica, CA: RAND, 2008), 61.

63. Dalia M. Spektor, *"Oil Well Fires" in A Review of the Scientific Literature as it Pertains to Gulf War Illnesses*, Vol. 6. (Santa Monica, CA: RAND, 1998), ix.

64. George P. Johnson, "Deployment Health and Environmental Exposures in OEF/OIF," Power Point, 29 January 2007. www.tricare.mil/conferences/2007/Mon/M109.ppt (accessed 21 October 2011).

65. U.S. Medicine, "Legislators Express Concern Regarding Environmental Hazards," *U.S. Medicine*, November 2009, http://www.usmedicine.com/articles/legislators-express-concern-regarding-environmental-hazards.html / (accessed 8 October 2011).

66. Michael R. Peterson, "Testimony," Senate Veterans Affairs Committee, 8 October 2009. http://veterans.senate.gov/hearings.cfm?action=release.display&release_id=b974df2c-0767-4d50-9caf-12cc16d5f198 (accessed 23 October 2011).

67. David E. Mosher, et. al., *Green Warriors - Army Environmental Considerations for Contingency Operations from Planning Through Post-Conflict* (Santa Monica, CA: RAND, 2008), 62.

68. VA Public Health, Operations Enduring Freedom and Iraqi Freedom (OEF/OIF) Hazardous Exposures, 19 May 2011, http://www.publichealth.va.gov/exposures/oefoif/index.asp (accessed 11 October 2011).

69. U.S. Medicine, "Legislators Express Concern Regarding Environmental Hazards," *U.S. Medicine*, November 2009, http://www.usmedicine.com/articles/legislators-express-concern-regarding-environmental-hazards.html / (accessed 8 October 2011).

70. David E. Mosher, et. al., *Green Warriors - Army Environmental Considerations for Contingency Operations from Planning Through Post-Conflict* (Santa Monica, CA: RAND, 2008), 202.

71. Ibid., 192.

72. Ibid., 199.

73. VA Public Health, Operations Enduring Freedom and Iraqi Freedom (OEF/OIF) Hazardous Exposures, 19 May 2011, http://www.publichealth.va.gov/exposures/oefoif/index.asp (accessed 11 October 2011).

74. David E. Mosher, et. al., *Green Warriors - Army Environmental Considerations for Contingency Operations from Planning Through Post-Conflict* (Santa Monica, CA: RAND, 2008), 92.

75. Central Intelligence Agency, "The World Factbook: Mexico," CIA, 27 September 2011, https://www.cia.gov/library/publications/the-world-factbook/geos/mx.html (accessed 9 October 2011).

76. U.S. Department of Justice, *National Drug Threat Assessment 2010*, (National Drug Intelligence Center, 2010).

77. Office of Environmental Health, Safety, and Toxicology, "Clandestine Drug Lab Cleanup." *Washington State Department of Health,* 5 July 2011, http://www.doh.wa.gov/ehp/cdl/ (accessed 10 October 2011).

78. KCI, "Cleaning Up Former Methamphetamine Labs," KCI: The Anti-Meth Site, http://www.kci.org/meth_info/meth_cleanup.htm (accessed 10 October 2011).

79. Office of Environmental Health, Safety, and Toxicology, "Clandestine Drug Lab Cleanup." *Washington State Department of Health, 5* July 2011, http://www.doh.wa.gov/ehp/cdl/ (accessed 10 October 2011).

80. Public Health Seattle and King County, *Illegal Drug Lab Cleanups*, 20 September 2011, http://www.kingcounty.gov/healthservices/health/ehs/toxic/methlabs.aspx (accessed 10 October 2011).

81. U.S. Department of Justice, *National Drug Threat Assessment 2010*, (National Drug Intelligence Center, 2010).

82. Office of Environmental Health, Safety, and Toxicology, "Clandestine Drug Lab Cleanup." *Washington State Department of Health, 5* July 2011, http://www.doh.wa.gov/ehp/cdl/ (accessed 10 October 2011).

83. KCI, "Cleaning Up Former Methamphetamine Labs," KCI: The Anti-Meth Site, http://www.kci.org/meth_info/meth_cleanup.htm (accessed 10 October 2011).

84. Associated Press, "Mexico Seizes Huge Warehouse of Meth Precursors," *CNS news, 21* July 2011. http://www.cnsnews.com/news/article/mexico-seizes-huge-warehouse-meth-precursors (accessed 10 October 2011).

85. Guillermo Foladori and Edgar Zayago Lau, "Tracking Nanotechnology in Mexico," *Nanotechnology Law and Business, Vol. 4, Issue 2*, 2007.

86. California Department of Toxic Substances Control, Nanotechnology, 3 June 2010, http://nanotech.law.asu.edu/Documents/2010/06/DTSC_444_3013.pdf (accessed 26 October 2011).

87. National Institute for Occupational Safety and Health (NIOSH), *"Interim Guidance for Medical Screening and Hazard Surveillance for Workers Potentially Exposed to Engineered Nanoparticles."* Current Intelligence Bulletin 60, Centers for Disease Control and Prevention, 2009.

88. American Council for the United Nations University. *Potential Environmental Pollution and Health Hazards Resulting from Possible Military Uses of Nanotechnology with Implications for Research Priorities Helpful to Prevent and/or Reduce Such Pollution and Hazards*, Millenium Project, February 2005.

89. California Council on Science and Technology, "Nanotechnology in California," January 2010, http://www.ccst.us/publications/2010/2010Nano.pdf (accessed 26 October 2011).

90. Fernando Bejarano González, et. al., *Burning Our Health: Hazardous Waste Incineration in Cement Kilns in Mexico* (Austin, TX: Texas Center for Policy Studies, 1998).

91. Environmental Protection Agency, *State of the Border Region - Indicators Report 2005,* EPA-160-R-06-001, (EPA, 2006), 10.

92. Fernando Bejarano González, et. al., *Burning Our Health: Hazardous Waste Incineration in Cement Kilns in Mexico* (Austin, TX: Texas Center for Policy Studies, 1998).

93. Ibid.

94. Associated Press, "Critics Oppose Border Patrol Herbicide Plan," *Fox News*, 24 March 2009. http://www.foxnews.com/wires/2009Mar24/0,4670,BorderPatrolPoison,00.html (accessed 10 October 2011).

95. Elliot C. McLaughlin, "Feds' Plan to Poison Banks of Rio Grande Stalled." *CNN*, 25 March 2009, http://articles.cnn.com/2009-03-25/us/mexico.border.herbicide_1_border-patrol-rio-grande-us-mexico-border?_s=PM:US (accessed 10 October 2011).

96. Associated Press, "Critics Oppose Border Patrol Herbicide Plan," *Fox News*, 24 March 2009. http://www.foxnews.com/wires/2009Mar24/0,4670,BorderPatrolPoison,00.html (accessed 10 October 2011).

97. Tyler Schenk-Wasson, "Herbicide Spraying in Texas: Border Patrol vs. Locals." *AllGov,* 11 April 2011,http://www.allgov.com/Controversies/ViewNews/Herbicide_Spraying_in_Texas__Border _Patrol_vs_Locals_90411 (accessed 10 October 2011).

98. U.S. Medicine, "Legislators Express Concern Regarding Environmental Hazards," *U.S. Medicine*, November 2009, http://www.usmedicine.com/articles/legislators-express-concern-regarding-environmental-hazards.html / (accessed 8 October 2011).

99. David E. Mosher, et. al., *Green Warriors - Army Environmental Considerations for Contingency Operations from Planning Through Post-Conflict* (Santa Monica, CA: RAND, 2008).

BIBLIOGRAPHY

Centers for Disease Control and Prevention. *Dengue in Tropical and Subtropical Regions.* September 15, 2011. http://wwwnc.cdc.gov/travel/notices/outbreak-notice/dengue-tropical-sub-tropical.htm (accessed October 19, 2011).

111th Congress. "Bill Text Versions: H.R. 2647." *Library of Congress Thomas.* January 6, 2009. http://thomas.loc.gov/cgi-bin/query/z?c111:H.R.2647:# (accessed October 19, 2011).

Advameg Inc. *Environment.* 2007. http://www.city-data.com/world-cities/Mexico-City-Environment.html (accessed October 9, 2011).

American Cancer Society. *Agent Orange and Cancer.* June 25, 2010. http://www.cancer.org/Cancer/CancerCauses/OtherCarcinogens/IntheWorkplace/agent-orange-and-cancer (accessed October 11, 2011).

American Council for the United Nations University. *Potential Environmental Pollution and Health Hazards Resulting from Possible Military Uses of Nanotechnology with Implications for Research Priorities Helpful to Prevent and/or Reduce Such Pollution and Hazards .* Millenium Project, www.prospective-foresight.com/IMG/doc/MP_nanotech_report.doc: American Council for the United Nations University, 2005, www.prospective-foresight.com/IMG/doc/MP_nanotech_report.doc.

Arizona Department of Health Services. *Border Infectious Disease Surveillance (BIDS).* August 24, 2011. http://www.azdhs.gov/diro/borderhealth/bids.htm (accessed October 10, 2011).

Associated Press. "Critics Oppose Border Patrol Herbicide Plan." *Fox News.* March 24, 2009. http://www.foxnews.com/wires/2009Mar24/0,4670,BorderPatrolPoison,00.html (accessed October 10, 2011).

—. "Mexico Seizes Huge Warehouse of Meth Precursors." *CNS news.* July 21, 2011. http://www.cnsnews.com/news/article/mexico-seizes-huge-warehouse-meth-precursors (accessed October 10, 2011).

Barranon, A., and A. Juanico. *Nanotechnology in the Northern Border of Mexico.* http://somi.ccadet.unam.mx/nanomex2010/memorias/95-AB_memoria.pdf: Nano Mex 2010 Conference, 2010.

Bender et. al, Stephen O. *Disaster, Planning and Development: Managing Natural Hazards to Reduce Loss.* http://oas.org/dsd/publications/Unit/oea54e/begin.htm#Contents, Washington, D.C.: Organization of American States, 1990.

Blacksmith Institute. *The World's Worst Polluted Places: The Top Ten of the Dirty Thirty.* http://www.blacksmithinstitute.org/wwpp2007/finalReport2007.pdf: Blacksmith Institute, 2007.

Borderland Beat. *Ascensión Chihuahua Police Force Resigns After Drug-Gang Attacks* . August 5, 2011. http://www.borderlandbeat.com/2011/08/ascension-chihuahua-police-force.html (accessed October 9, 2011).

California Council on Science and Technology. "Nanotechnology in California." January 2010. http://www.ccst.us/publications/2010/2010Nano.pdf (accessed October 26, 2011).

California Department of Toxic Substances Control. *Nanotechnology.* June 3, 2010. http://nanotech.law.asu.edu/Documents/2010/06/DTSC_444_3013.pdf (accessed October 26, 2011).

Carter, Dean E. et. al. "Environmental Health and Hazardous Waste Issues Related to the U.S.-Mexico Border." *Environmental Health Perspectives*, June 1996: http://www.ncbi.nlm.nih.gov/pmc/articles/PMC1469378/pdf/envhper00337-0018.pdf.

Castaneda, Mario. *Binational Water Quality Monitoring Activities Along the Arizona-Sonora Border Region.* http://acwi.gov/monitoring/conference/98proceedings/Papers/34-CAST.html: Arizona Department of Environmental Quality, 1998.

Centers for Disease Control and Prevention . *Outbreak Notice Update: Dengue in Tropical and Subtropical Regions.* September 15, 2011. http://wwwnc.cdc.gov/travel/notices/outbreak-notice/dengue-tropical-sub-tropical.htm (accessed October 24, 2011).

Centers for Disease Control and Prevention. "Environmental Hazards and Health Effects." *CDC.* July 27, 2011. http://www.cdc.gov/nceh/ehhe/ (accessed October 10, 2011).

—. *U.S.-Mexico Border Environmental Health Issues.* http://www.cdc.gov/nceh/hsb/borderhealth/#pubs (accessed October 10, 2011).

—. *U.S.-Mexico Border Environmental Health Issues.* http://www.cdc.gov/nceh/hsb/borderhealth/#pubs (accessed October 10, 2011).

Central Intelligence Agency. *The World Factbook: Mexico.* September 27, 2011. https://www.cia.gov/library/publications/the-world-factbook/geos/mx.html (accessed October 9, 2011).

Centurion Risk Assessment Services. *Country Risks Assessments - Mexico.* 2011. http://www.centurionsafety.net/Countries/Mexico.html (accessed October 12, 2011).

Clendenon, Cindy, and William Atkins. "Pollution of the Ocean by Sewage, Nutrients, and Chemicals ." *Water Encyclopedia, Advameg Inc.* 2011. http://www.waterencyclopedia.com/Po-Re/Pollution-of-the-Ocean-by-Sewage-Nutrients-and-Chemicals.html (accessed October 10, 2011).

Commission for Environmental Cooperation of North America. "DDT No Longer Used in North America." *Commission for Environmental Cooperation.* April 2003. http://www.cec.org/Storage/50/4285_DDT_en.pdf (accessed October 10, 2011).

Connolly, Priscilla. "Mexico City: Our Common Future?" *Environment and Urbanization, Vol. 11, No. 1*, April 1999: http://eau.sagepub.com/content/11/1/53.full.pdf.

Danopoulos, Constantine P. "Economic Measurements and Quality of Life in Mexico." *Journal of Political & Military Sociology, Winter, Vol. 32 Issue 2*, 2004: http://web.ebscohost.com/ehost/detail?sid=053aa3a5-ca89-4765-b640-da2f077e4f1f%40sessionmgr114&vid=1&hid=106&bdata=JnNpdGU9ZWhvc3QtbGl2ZQ%3d%3d#db=mth&AN=19403072.

DoD Deployment Health Clinical Center. *Information on Deployment-Related Exposures.* http://www.pdhealth.mil/dcs/deploymentexposure.asp#VAC (accessed October 8, 2011).

Environmental Protection Agency. *Border 2020: U.S.-Mexico Environmental Program .* Draft for public comment, http://www.epa.gov/usmexicoborder/docs/2020/border2020-draft-framework.pdf: EPA, September 5, 2011.

Environmental Protection Agency. "Data Tables for the State of the Border Region Indicators Report." http://www.epa.gov/usmexicoborder/docs/bitf_table.pdf, 2005.

—. "Environmental Pollution." *Oracle Education Foundation.* 1998. http://library.thinkquest.org/C001611/pollution.html (accessed October 10, 2011).

—. "Protecting Human Health in the Border Region." *EPA, U.S.-Mexico Border 2012.* August 4, 2011. http://www.epa.gov/usmexicoborder/success/tx-nm-chihuahua/tx-elpaso-climate-health.html (accessed October 10, 2011).

Environmental Protection Agency. "State of the Border Region." Indicators Report 2005, http://www.epa.gov/usmexicoborder/indicators/05report/SBR_2005_English.pdf, 2006.

—. *State of the Border Region Indicators Report 2005.* March 20, 2007. http://epa.gov/border2012/indicators/water.html (accessed October 9, 2011).

—. *U.S.-Mexico Border 2012: People Along the Border.* October 12, 2010. http://www.epa.gov/border2012/framework/people.html (accessed October 9, 2011).

Environmental Protection Agency. *U.S.-Mexico Environmental Program: Border 2012.* Implementation and Mid-Term Report 2007, EPA, 2007, http://www.epa.gov/usmexicoborder/docs/implementation_2007_eng.pdf (accessed October 11, 2011).

Falcone, Michael. "Rick Perry Says Drug War 'May Require Our Military in Mexico'." *ABC News.* October 1, 2011. http://abcnews.go.com/blogs/politics/2011/10/rick-perry-says-drug-war-may-require-our-military-in-mexico/ (accessed October 10, 2011).

Flakus, Greg. "SARS/Mexico." *GlobalSecurity.org.* April 30, 2003. http://www.globalsecurity.org/military/library/news/2003/04/mil-030430-3d1954c9.htm (accessed October 10, 2011).

Foladori, Guillermo, and Edgar Zayago Lau. "Tracking Nanotechnology in Mexico." *Nanotechnology Law and Business, Vol. 4, Issue 2,* 2007: http://www.nanolabweb.com/index.cfm/action/main.default.viewArticle/articleID/194/CFID/627091/CFTOKEN/33862493/.

Fraser, C. Gerald. "History of the North American Free Trade Agreement (NAFTA)." *Nafta's environmental problems.* January 22, 1996. http://www.hartford-hwp.com/archives/40/022.html (accessed October 9, 2011).

Friedman, George. "Mexico: On the Road to a Failed State?" *Stratfor Global Intelligence.* May 13, 2008. http://www.stratfor.com/weekly/mexico_road_failed_state (accessed October 10, 2011).

Gallagher, Kevin P. *Free Trade and the Environment: Mexico, NAFTA, and Beyond.* http://www.ase.tufts.edu/gdae/Pubs/rp/NAFTAEnviroKGAmerProgSep04.pdf: Americas Program, Interhemispheric Resource Center, 2004.

GlobalSecurity. *Early Warning Infectious Disease Surveillance (EWIDS).* July 13, 2011. http://www.globalsecurity.org/security/systems/ewids.htm (accessed October 10, 2011).

—. *Environment.* September 7, 2011. http://www.globalsecurity.org/military/world/mexico/environment.htm (accessed October 10, 2011).

Godoy, Emilio. "Mexico: Little Oversight of Radiation Sources." *Global Issues.* May 13, 2011. http://www.globalissues.org/news/2011/05/13/9648 (accessed October 10, 2011).

—. "Villagers Complain of Health Risks from Nuclear Plant." *Inter Press Service (IPS).* March 30, 2011. http://ipsnews.net/news.asp?idnews=55060 (accessed October 10, 2011).

González, Fernando Bejarano et. al. *Burning Our Health: Hazardous Waste Incineration in Cement Kilns in Mexico.* Translation, http://www.texascenter.org/publications/kiln.htm: Texas Center for Policy Studies, 1998.

Gosselin, Pierre, Chris Furgal, and Alfonso Ruiz. *Environmental Public Health Indicators for the U.S.-Mexico Border Region.* Concept Document, http://www.fep.paho.org/english/env/Indicadores/Environmental%20Public%20Health%20Indicators.pdf: Pan American Health Organization, July 2001.

Gross, Robert A., and W. Thomas Broadwater. *Occupational Health: The Soldier and the Industrial Base, Chapter 6, Health Hazard Assessments.* http://www.bordeninstitute.army.mil/published_volumes/occ_health/OHch6.pdf: Department of the Army, Office of The Surgeon General, Borden Institute, 1993.

Gutierrez, David. "Border Agents to Dump Agent Orange-Like Chemical to Kill All Plant Life Among U.S.-Mexico Border." *Republic of Health.* July 3, 2009. http://republicofhealth.wordpress.com/tag/mexico-border/#!/page/1 (accessed October 10, 2011).

Honda, Mike et.al. *Nanotechnology: Thinking Big about Thinking Small.* Blue Ribbon Task Force for California, http://www.bayeconfor.org/media/files/pdf/brtfn_12_19_05.pdf: Bay Area Council Economic Institute, 2005.

Idaho Department of Health and Welfare. *Clandestine Drug (Meth) Lab Cleanup Program of Idaho.* 2009. http://www.healthandwelfare.idaho.gov/Health/EnvironmentalHealth/MethamphetamineClandestineLabCleanup/tabid/183/Default.aspx (accessed October 10, 2011).

Ip, Regina. "Environmental Issues Hurting Communities in the U.S.-Mexico Border Region." *La Prensa San Diego.* June 25, 2010. http://laprensa-sandiego.org/stories/environmental-issues-hurting-communities-in-the-u-s-mexico-border-region/ (accessed October 9, 2011).

Johannessen, Lars Mikkel, and Gabriela Boyer. *Observations of Solid Waste Landfills in Developing Countries: Africa, Asia, and Latin America.* http://www.worldbank.org/urban/solid_wm/erm/CWG%20folder/uwp3.pdf: Urban Development Division, The World Bank, 1999.

Johnson, George P. *Deployment Health and Environmental Exposures in OEF/OIF.* January 29, 2007. www.tricare.mil/conferences/2007/Mon/M109.ppt (accessed October 21, 2011).

KCI. "Cleaning Up Former Methamphetamine Labs." *KCI: The Anti-Meth Site.* http://www.kci.org/meth_info/meth_cleanup.htm (accessed October 10, 2011).

Kennedy, Kelly. "Lung Disease of Soldier Linked to Burn Pits." *Military Times.* June 30, 2009. http://www.militarytimes.com/news/2009/06/military_burnpits_lungs_063009w/ (accessed October 9, 2011).

Kourous, George. "Environmental Problems and Cross-border Activism ." *Information Services Latin America (ISLA).* 1999. http://isla.igc.org/Features/Border/mex3.html (accessed October 9, 2011).

Landa, Rosalva, Jorge Meave, and Julia Carabias. "Environmental Deterioration in Rural Mexico: An Examination of the Concept." *Ecological Applications, Vol. 7, No. 1,* 1997: http://www.jstor.org/pss/2269426?searchUrl=%2Faction%2FdoBasicSearch%3FQuery%3Denvironmental%2Bproblems%2BMexico%26acc%3Doff%26wc%3Don&Search=yes&.

Lennard, Natasha. *Is our debt to China a national security risk?* May 10, 2011.
http://www.salon.com/news/politics/war_room/2011/05/10/china_debt_national_security
(accessed September 10, 2011).

Lopez-Carrilo et. al, Lizabeth. "Is DDT Use a Public Health Problem in Mexico?" *Environmental Health Perspectives,Vol. 104, No. 6*, June 1996:
http://ehp03.niehs.nih.gov/article/fetchArticle.action?articleURI=info%3Adoi%2F10.1289%2Fehp.96
104584.

Lydersen, Kari. "Environmental and Health Concerns Don't Stop at U.S.-Mexican Border." *Surfrider Foundation.* 2009. http://sandiego.surfrider.org/environmental-and-health-concerns-dont-stop-at-u-s-mexican-border (accessed October 10, 2011).

Malstrom, Howard A., and Wayne R. Jordan. *Environmental Issues of the U.S.-Mexico Border Region.*
A Workshop Summary,
http://repository.tamu.edu/bitstream/handle/1969.1/6166/tr166.pdf?sequence=1: Texas Water
Resources Institute, 1994.

Maranon-Pimentel, Boris. "Economic Costs of Water-related Health Problems in Mexico:
Deficiencies in Potable Water Services and the Costs of Treatment of Diarrhoeas." *Water Resources Development, Vol. 25, No. 1, 65–80*, March 2009: http://www.thirdworldcentre.org/boris2009.pdf.

McCaffrey, Barry R., and Robert H. Scales. *Texas Border Security: A Strategic Military Assessment.*
Commissioned by Texas Department of Agriculture and Department of Public Safety,
http://www.texasagriculture.gov/vgn/tda/files/1848/46982_Final%20Report-
Texas%20Border%20Security.pdf: Colgen LP, 2011.

McCartor et. al, Andrew. *World's Worst Pollution Problems Report 2010.*
http://www.worstpolluted.org/files/FileUpload/files/2010/WWPP-Report-2010-Top-Six-Toxic-
Threats-Web.pdf: Blacksmith Institute, 2011.

McLaughlin, Eliott C. "Feds' plan to poison banks of Rio Grande stalled." *CNN.* March 25, 2009.
http://articles.cnn.com/2009-03-25/us/mexico.border.herbicide_1_border-patrol-rio-grande-us-
mexico-border?_s=PM:US (accessed October 10, 2011).

Melesio, Lucina. "DDT found in children from Mexico and Central America." *Environmental News Network (ENN).* February 18, 2010. http://www.enn.com/ecosystems/article/41028 (accessed October 10, 2011).

Merrill, Tim L., and Ramón Miró (editors). *Mexico: A Country Study.* Study,
http://countrystudies.us/mexico/51.htm: GPO for the Library of Congress, 1996.

Mosher, David E. et. al. *Green Warriors - Army Environmental Considerations for Contingency Operations from Planning Through Post-Conflict.*

http://www.aepi.army.mil/docs/whatsnew/RAND_MG632.pdf, Santa Monica, CA: Rand Corporation, 2008.

Mrela, Christopher, and Clare Torres. *Deaths from Exposure to Excessive Natural Heat Occuring in Arizona* . http://www.azdhs.gov/plan/report/heat/heat09.pdf: Arizona Department of Health Services, 2010.

National Institute for Occupational Safety and Health (NIOSH). *Interim Guidance for Medical Screening and Hazard Surveillance for Workers Potentially Exposed to Engineered Nanoparticles.* Current Intelligence Bulletin 60, http://www.cdc.gov/niosh/docs/2009-116/pdfs/2009-116.pdf: Centers for Disease Control and Prevention, 2009.

National Research Council, Committee for Oversight and Assessment of U.S. Department of Energy Project Management. *The Owner's Role in Project Risk Management, Chapter 5, Risk Mitigation.* http://www.nap.edu/openbook.php?record_id=11183&page=41: The National Academies Press, 2005.

New Mexico State University. "Dengue on the Loose." *Frontera NorteSur.* July 25, 2010. http://fnsnews.nmsu.edu/2010/07/25/dengue-on-the-loose/ (accessed October 11, 2011).

O'Connor, Anne-Marie. "Mexico City Drastically Reduced Air Pollutants Since 1990s." *The Washington Post.* April 1, 2010. http://www.washingtonpost.com/wp-dyn/content/article/2010/03/31/AR2010033103614.html?sid=ST2010033103622 (accessed October 12, 2011).

OEHHA. "Methamphetamine Clean Up Fact Sheet." *Office of Environmental Health Hazard Assessment, California EPA.* 2007. http://oehha.ca.gov/public_info/clanlabs.html#download (accessed October 10, 2011).

Office of Environmental Health, Safety, and Toxicology. "Clandestine Drug Lab Cleanup." *Washington State Department of Health.* July 5, 2011. http://www.doh.wa.gov/ehp/cdl/ (accessed October 10, 2011).

Oil and Gas Author. *Environmental Issues in Mexico.* August 24, 2006. http://www.oilgasarticles.com/articles/212/1/Environmental-Issues-in-Mexico/Page1.html (accessed August 9, 2011).

Pan American Health Organization. *Environmental Health Indicators Workshop: U.S.-Mexico Border.* http://www.fep.paho.org/english/env/Indicadores/McAllen/EHI%20McAllen%20Final%20Report.pdf: World Health Organization, 2002.

—. *Health Situation Analysis and Trends Summary - Mexico.* 2000. http://www.paho.org/english/dd/ais/cp_484.htm (accessed October 11, 2011).

Peterson, Michael R., Chief Consultant, VA Environmental Health Strategic Healthcare Group. *Senate ⬚eterans Affairs Committee hearing.* October 8, 2009. http://veterans.senate.gov/hearings.cfm?action=release.display&release_id=b974df2c-0767-4d50-9caf-12cc16d5f198 (accessed October 23, 2011).

Postlewaite, R. Craig. *Environmental Health Threats in Theater - ⬚essons ⬚earned.* 2010 Military Health System Conference, http://www.health.mil/Libraries/2010_MHS_Conference_Presentations_Jan_27/W17_C_Postlewaite.pdf: DoD(HA)/Force Health Protection and Readiness Programs, January 26, 2010.

Public Health Seattle and King County. *Illegal Drug ⬚a⬚ Cleanups.* September 20, 2011. http://www.kingcounty.gov/healthservices/health/ehs/toxic/methlabs.aspx (accessed October 10, 2011).

Rand Corporation. *Examining Possi⬚le Causes of Gulf War Illness.* http://www.rand.org/content/dam/rand/pubs/research_briefs/2005/RAND_RB7544.pdf: Rand Corporation, 2005.

Ross, John. "Dangers in Paradise - Environmental Problems in Mexico." *Sierra*, July-Aug 1992: http://findarticles.com/p/articles/mi_m1525/is_n4_v77/ai_12449677/ accessed October 10, 2011.

Sanchez, Roberto A. "Water quality problems in Nogales, Sonora." *Environmental Health Perspectives*, February 1995: http://www.ncbi.nlm.nih.gov/pmc/articles/PMC1519322/.

Sapkota et. al, Sanjeeb. "Unauthorized Border Crossings and Migrant Deaths: Arizona, New Mexico, and El Paso, Texas, 2002–2003." *American ⬚ournal of Pu⬚lic Health, ⬚ol ⬚⬚, No. ⬚*, July 2006: http://www.borderhealth.org/files/res_671.pdf.

Schenk-Wasson, Tyler. "Herbicide Spraying in Texas: Border Patrol vs. Locals." *AllGov.* April 11, 2011. http://www.allgov.com/Controversies/ViewNews/Herbicide_Spraying_in_Texas__Border_Patrol_vs_Locals_90411 (accessed October 10, 2011).

Sibbald, Barbara. "DDT Use Finally Eliminated in North America." *Canadian Medical Association ⬚ournal.* May 14, 2002. http://www.cmaj.ca/content/166/10/1322.1.full (accessed October 24, 2011).

Siebe, Claus, and José Luis Macías. "Volcanic Hazards in the Mexico City Metropolitan Area from Eruptions at Popocatépetl, Nevado de Toluca, and Jocotitlán stratovolcanoes and monogenetic scoria cones in the Sierra Chichinautzin Volcanic Field." *Geological Society of America, Special Papers, ⬚ol. ⬚⬚⬚*, 2006: http://specialpapers.gsapubs.org/content/402/253.short.

Spektor, Dalia M. "Oil Well Fires." In *A Review of the Scientific ⬚iterature as it Pertains to Gulf War Illnesses*, by Rand Corporation, Vol. 6. http://www.gulflink.osd.mil/library/rand_owf.pdf: Rand Corporation, 1998.

31

Stone, Hannah. "Army Busts Huge Meth Lab in South Mexico." *In Sight: Organized Crime in the Americas.* May 30, 2011. http://insightcrime.org/insight-latest-news/item/1000-army-busts-huge-meth-lab-in-south-mexico (accessed October 10, 2011).

Tran, Nga L. et. al. "Environmental Health Risk Assessment Methodology." *⊠ohns Hopkins AP⊠ Technical Digest, ⊠ol. ⊠⊠, No. ⊠*, 1999: http://www.jhuapl.edu/techdigest/TD/td2003/tran.pdf.

U.S. Army Center for Health Promotion and Preventive Medicine. "Guide for Deployed Preventive Medicine Personnel on Health Risk Management." Technical Guide 248, http://phc.amedd.army.mil/PHC%20Resource%20Library/TG%20248%20Guide%20for%20Deployed%20Preventive%20Medicine%20Personnel%20on%20Health%20Risk%20Management.pdf, 2001.

U.S. Army Personnel Health Command . *Environmental Health Risk Assessment and Chemical Exposure Guidelines for Deployed Military Personnel ⊠TG ⊠⊠⊠⊠* http://phc.amedd.army.mil/PHC%20Resource%20Library/TG230.pdf, 2010.

U.S. Army Public Health Command . *Environmental Health Risk Assessment and Chemical Exposure Guidelines for Deployed Military Personnel.* Technical Guide 230, http://phc.amedd.army.mil/PHC%20Resource%20Library/TG230.pdf: U.S. Army, 2010.

U.S. Army Public Health Command. *Deployment Environmental Surveillance Program ⊠DESP⊠* http://phc.amedd.army.mil/organization/institute/dhrm/Pages/DESP.aspx (accessed October 12, 2011).

—. *Environmental Health Risk Assessment .* http://phc.amedd.army.mil/topics/envirohealth/hrasm/Pages/EnvironmentalHealthRiskAssessment.aspx (accessed October 8, 2011).

U.S. Commercial Service. "Klean Industries." *Environmental Services in Mexico.* October 14, 2008. http://www.kleanindustries.com/s/PressReleases.asp?ReportID=325076 (accessed October 9, 2011).

U.S. Department of Defense. *DOD Instruction Num⊠er ⊠⊠⊠⊠.⊠⊠, Deployment Health.* August 11, 2006. http://www.dtic.mil/whs/directives/corres/pdf/649003p.pdf (accessed October 25, 2011).

U.S. Department of Justice. *National Drug Threat Assessment ⊠⊠⊠⊠.* http://www.justice.gov/ndic/pubs38/38661/38661p.pdf: National Drug Intelligence Center, 2010.

U.S. Department of State. *Background Note: Mexico.* December 14, 2010. http://www.state.gov/r/pa/ei/bgn/35749.htm (accessed October 9, 2011).

U.S. Geological Survey. "Historic World Earthquakes." *USGS Earth⊠uake Hazards Program.* March 11, 2011. http://earthquake.usgs.gov/earthquakes/world/historical_country.php (accessed October 10, 2011).

—. *Human Health.* February 25, 2011. http://health.usgs.gov/ (accessed October 10, 2011).

—. "Mexico Earthquake Information." *USGS Earth□uake Hazards Program.* October 2011. http://earthquake.usgs.gov/earthquakes/world/index.php?region=Mexico (accessed October 10, 2011).

—. "Mexico Seismic Hazard Map." *USGS Earth□uake Hazards Program .* October 26, 2009. http://earthquake.usgs.gov/earthquakes/world/mexico/gshap.php (accessed October 10, 2011).

—. *U.S. - Mexico Border Environmental Health Initiative □BEHI□.* 21 January, 2011. http://borderhealth.cr.usgs.gov/projectindex.html (accessed October 10, 2011).

U.S. Medicine. *□egislators Express Concern Regarding Environmental Hazards.* November 2009. http://www.usmedicine.com/articles/legislators-express-concern-regarding-environmental-hazards.html (accessed October 8, 2011).

U.S. Senate Commitee on Veterans' Affairs. *Statement of Michael R. Peterson, □A Environmental Health Strategic Healthcare Group.* October 8, 2009. http://veterans.senate.gov/hearings.cfm?action=release.display&release_id=b974df2c-0767-4d50-9caf-12cc16d5f198 (accessed October 11, 2011).

U.S-Mexico Border Health Commission, New Mexico Border Health. *Demographic Profile of U.S.-Mexico Border.* 2000. http://www.nmsu.edu/~bhcom/ (accessed October 9, 2011).

USAID. *Country Health Statistical Report: Mexico.* http://dolphn.aimglobalhealth.org/pdf/Mexico.pdf: United States Agency for International Development, January 2011.

—. *Environmental Health.* September 28, 2011. http://www.usaid.gov/our_work/global_health/eh/index.html# (accessed October 9, 2011).

VA Public Health. *Gulf War □eterans' Illnesses.* September 15, 2011. http://www.publichealth.va.gov/exposures/gulfwar/index.asp (accessed October 11, 2011).

—. *Hazardous Exposures.* September 29, 2011. http://www.publichealth.va.gov/exposures/index.asp (accessed October 08, 2011).

—. *Operations Enduring Freedom and Ira□i Freedom □OEF□OIF□Hazardous Exposures.* May 19, 2011. http://www.publichealth.va.gov/exposures/oefoif/index.asp (accessed October 11, 2011).

—. *When and Where Agent Orange Was Sprayed in □ietnam.* August 19, 2011. http://www.publichealth.va.gov/exposures/agentorange/diseases.asp#veterans (accessed October 24, 2011).

Veterans Benefits Administration. *The Agent Orange Settlement Fund.* November 8, 2009.
http://www.vba.va.gov/bln/21/benefits/herbicide/AOno2.htm (accessed October 25, 2011).

War Related Illness & Injury Study Center. "Medically Unexplained Symptoms: A Resource for
Veterans, Service Members, and Their Families." *A Public Health.* August 2011.
http://www.warrelatedillness.va.gov/WARRELATEDILLNESS/education/factsheets/medically-
unexplained-symptoms.pdf (accessed October 10, 2011).

Warner, David C., and Lauren R. Jahnke. *U.S.-Mexico Border Health Issues: The Texas Rio Grande
alley.* http://www.uthscsa.edu/RCHWS/Reports/NAFTA2.pdf: University of Texas Health Science
Center at San Antonio, 2003.